GASSIRE'S LUTE

GASSIRE'S LUTE

A WEST AFRICAN EPIC

Translation, adaptation and essay by
ALTA JABLOW

Illustrations by Leo and Diane Dillon

WAVELAND
PRESS, INC.
Prospect Heights, Illinois

For information about this book, write or call:

Waveland Press, Inc.
P.O. Box 400
Prospect Heights, Illinois 60070
(708) 634-0081

Translation and adaptation copyright © 1971 by Alta Jablow from Leo Frobenius, *Spielmannsgeschichten der Sahel,* Atlantis, Bd. VI, Jena: Diederichs Verlag, 1921
1991 reissued with changes by Waveland Press, Inc.

Illustrations copyright © 1971 by Leo and Diane Dillon

ISBN 0-88133-543-6

Printed in the United States of America

7   6   5   4   3

To Carl Withers

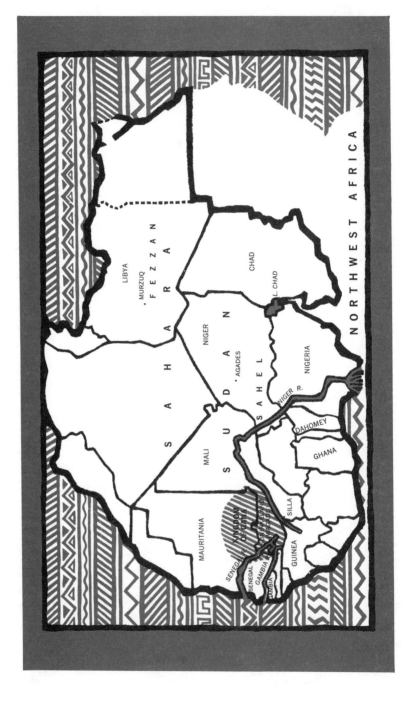

INTRODUCTION

Gassire's Lute is a legend from the Sudan of West Africa, which is, in its present form, at least as old as the seventeenth century. It is a stirring tale of wars and heroes — one of the few surviving pieces of a still earlier and greater epic, the *dausi*. The poem was sung or chanted by the bards or *diaru* of the Soninke people to the accompaniment of drumming or the strains of a calabash guitar. It tells of Gassire, the warrior son of the ruling family of Dierra, who renounced his noble birth to become the first Soninke bard.

Most of the *dausi* has been lost over the course of time, but it was originally a long, continuous epic that chronicled the legendary history of the Soninke. Its major theme centered on the rise and fall of their city-state, Wagadu. According to the legend, Wagadu existed at four different periods — each time the Soninke settled in their beloved Sahel as a free and autonomous people. *Gassire's Lute* tells of the fall of Dierra, the first Wagadu.

There is little real information concerning the earliest history of the Soninke. It is known that they were the rulers of the fabulously wealthy Sudanese Kingdom of Ghana (Gana), the third incarnation of Wagadu. From the fourth to the thirteenth centuries A.D., Ghana controlled the all-important Saharan trade routes and was the most prosperous and powerful state in West Africa. After the

7

thirteenth century, the power of Ghana was shattered and the Soninke dispersed: some became mercenary soldiers or bards; others settled as farmers, tradesmen, or herders in the states of kindred tribes all over Senegambia (Senegal-Gambia region) and the Upper Niger. This is, more or less, their condition today, but there is an area in the Western Sahel, still called Wagadu, where the Soninke live in greater numbers and which they consider their homeland.

The Soninke of the *dausi* are more akin to the noble rulers of early Ghana than to the peasants and tradesmen of today. In fact, they bear a most striking resemblance to the nobles and knights of medieval Europe. Like them, the Soninke *horro*, members of the hereditary nobility, were warriors, fighting for their lands, their women, their lords, and, above all, for honor and fame. Like the European knights of the *chansons de geste* and the sagas, the *horro* were highborn, supremely conscious of their nobility and the purity of their bloodlines. They rode spirited horses, loved beautiful women, and lived in walled and fortified castles. When the *horro* fought men of standing equal to their own, such as the *Burdama* (Tuareg) warriors, they engaged in single combat — champion against champion — battling to the death with a sword in each hand. The *Boroma* (Fulani) were, however, slaves; they had been enslaved by the Soninke and the Tuareg as well. To indicate their contempt for such base-born rabble, the *horro* did not deign to use their swords, but drove them off as they would a pack of dogs, using only a leather whip or saddle girth.

Always at the side of the *horro* warrior rode his minstrel, his *diari*. Although lower in caste, the *diari* was not a mere servant, but a friend, wise counselor, and praise-singer. The chivalric code of honor did not permit the *horro* to boast

8

of his own deeds, but he could count upon his *diari* to do his boasting for him. In this way the *diari*'s songs extolling his lord's courage, daring, and devotion to honor spread all over the Western Sudan.

Some of these songs were incorporated into the *dausi*, others were cast in another form, the *pui*. These are individual, shorter pieces that exalt the feats of particular heroes. They were (and are) chanted in a regular meter, with a specifically set melodic accompaniment. A good *diari* must know both traditional forms, for they are still used as praise-songs and tales to enhance the prestige of contemporary men of importance. Their names are inserted in place of the traditional heroes, and events, and though not radically changed, may be omitted, their order reversed, or even transferred from one story to another.

Gassire's Lute was recorded in 1909 by Leo Frobenius, the German anthropologist. He heard it from a bard in Northern Dahomey, who claimed descent from the original family of Soninke bards that had migrated from the west a century before. I found it originally in an English prose version while searching out material on the bardic art to present to my class in African folklore at Brooklyn College. I tracked it back from *African Genesis* by Leo Frobenius and Douglas C. Fox (New York: Stackpole Sons, 1937) to the original source in the classic work by Frobenius published in Germany (*Spielmannsgeschichten der Sahel*, Atlantis, Bd. VI, Jena: Diederichs Verlag, 1921). Everything I knew about bardic art in West Africa and everything I could discover about its origin seemed to support my conviction that *Gassire's Lute* was a poem. In retranslating it from the German, I attempted to retrieve its poetic form. Lacking original text material (Frobenius nowhere includes the native text, nor gives any inkling of what it was like), I could be certain of very little concerning its meter, length of line, or stress. But the language and style of the narrative is of such a nature that, even without any change, it lent itself most readily to poetic transcription. Indeed, it seemed to require it.

As an example of the relatively unknown oral literatures of Africa, *Gassire's Lute* is rich in cultural and historical interest. For those who wish to know more of this background, an annotated glossary appears at the end of the book. But the poem can also be read and enjoyed simply as a beautiful and exciting story that once again demonstrates the universality of art and of human experience.

GASSIRE'S LUTE

Four times
    Wagadu rose.
    A great city, gleaming in the light of day.
Four times
    Wagadu fell.
    And disappeared from human sight.
        Once through vanity.
        Once through dishonesty.
        Once through greed.
        Once through discord.
Four times
    Wagadu changed her name.
        First she was called Dierra,
            then Agada,
            then Gana,
            then Silla.
Four times
    Wagadu turned about,
        facing first to the north,
        then to the west,
        then to the east,
        then to the south.

Four gates
    have always led into Wagadu.
    Thus men have always seen them.
      One to the north.
      One to the west.
      One to the east, and
      one to the south.
From these directions
Comes the strength of Wagadu.
Her power, which endures
Whether she be built of stone,
      of wood, or
      of earth.
Or whether she lives only as a shadow
In the memory and hopes of her children.
For in truth, Wagadu is not of stone,
      not of wood,
      nor of earth.
Wagadu is the strength
Which lives in the hearts of men.
Sometimes she becomes known
    when men's eyes see her,
    and their ears hear
  the clash of swords and the clang of shields.
Sometimes lost to view,
    when wearied and oppressed
    by the strife of men,
      she sleeps.
For the first time

Sleep came to Wagadu through vanity.
The second time through dishonesty.
The third time through greed.
The fourth time through discord.
Should Wagadu ever rise again,
    She will live with such power
  in the minds of men
      that she can never again be lost.
She will endure with such strength
    that vanity,
        dishonesty,
           greed,
              discord,
  can never again harm her.
Hoooh!
    Dierra, Agada, Gana, Silla!
Hoooh!
    Fasa!

Each time Wagadu was destroyed
  through the faults of men,
She reappeared with a greater splendor.
Vanity brought the song of the bards.
Dishonesty brought a shower of gold and precious stones.
Greed brought the art of writing to the women of Wagadu.
The fifth Wagadu will arise from discord
    to endure as the rain of the South,
      as the rocks of the Sahara.

Every man then will bear Wagadu in his heart.
Every woman will have Wagadu in her sons.
Hoooh!
    Dierra, Agada, Gana, Silla!
Hoooh!
    Fasa!

First, facing north,
    and called Dierra,
    ruled by Nganamba Fasa,
    Wagadu was lost through vanity.
Strong were the Fasa,
    and brave.
Day after day they fought
    against the Burdama
    and the Boroma slaves.
There was no end to the fighting.
And out of the fighting
    the strength of the Fasa grew.
All Nganamba's men were heroes.
All the women lovely,
    and proud of their men.
But the Fasa were growing old.
All who had not fallen
    in single combat with the Burdama
    were growing old.
Nganamba was very old.
Gassire, his son,

himself with eight sons,
    each son with sons.
Nganamba ruled over them,
    and over all the Fasa,
    and over the dog-like Boroma.
Because of him,
    because he grew so old,
Wagadu was lost.
The Boroma crept away,
    fleeing from the old Fasa's rule.
Again they became slaves to the Burdama.
And with the Burdama swords,
    together they conquered Wagadu,
    called Dierra.
Had Nganamba died sooner,
    would Wagadu have fallen for the first time?
Hoooh!
    Dierra, Agada, Gana, Silla!
Hoooh!
    Fasa!

Nganamba did not die.
A jackal gnawed at Gassire's heart.
Each day Gassire asked his heart:
    "When will Nganamba die?
    When will Gassire be king?"
Each day Gassire longed for the death of his father
  as a lover watches for the evening star to rise.

17

By day, when Gassire fought as a hero
        against the Burdama.
When he drove the treacherous Boroma before him
        with the leather girth of his saddle.
Then he thought only of the fighting,
                of his sword,
                of his shield,
                of his horse.
With the evening he rode into the city,
And sat in the circle of men and his sons.
Gassire heard the heroes praise his deeds,
But his heart was not with them.
His heart was full of misery and longing,
Longing for the shield of his father.
        The shield which he might carry
        only when his father was dead.
Longing for the sword of his father.
        The sword which he might draw
        only when he was king.
Each day Gassire's rage and longing grew.
Sleep passed him by.
Gassire lay, and a jackal gnawed at his heart.
Gassire lay, and anguish climbed into his throat.
One night he could no longer rest.
He sprang from his bed,
        leaving his house.
To the wise man, Kiekorro, went Gassire.
"Kiekorro!
        When will my father die?

When shall I carry his shield and sword?"
"Ah, Gassire!
    Nganamba will die soon enough.
    But you will never carry his sword and shield.
    Sword and shield will others inherit.
    You will carry a lute.
    And your lute shall cause the loss of Wagadu!
Ah, Gassire!"
"Kiekorro!
    You are not as wise as I thought.
    How can Wagadu be lost?
    Her heroes triumph daily.
    Your vision is false,
    And you are a fool.
Kiekorro!"
Then the wise old man spoke again:
"Ah, Gassire!
    You may not believe what I say now.
    But your fate will lead you
to the guinea hens in the fields.
    You will hear and understand
what they say.
    They will tell of your fate
and the fate of Wagadu."
Hoooh!
    Dierra, Agada, Gana, Silla!
Hoooh!
    Fasa!

Gassire was angry.
Again he went into battle with the Burdama.
He called to the heroes:
 "Stay here.
 Today I fight alone."
He rode forth to battle.
 Gassire hurled his spear.
 Gassire charged the Burdama.
 Gassire swung his sword.
 He struck down Burdama on the right.
 He struck them down on the left.
Gassire's sword was as a sickle mowing the grain.
The Burdama were stricken with terror.
They cried:
 "That is no Fasa.
 That is no mere hero.
 That is a Damo!"
The Burdama turned their horses.
The Burdama threw down their spears.
Each of them threw down his two spears,
 and they fled.
Gassire called his men.
Gassire said:
 "Gather up the spears."
They sang as they gathered the spears:
 "The Fasa are all heroes.
 Gassire has always been the greatest of the Fasa.
 Gassire has always done great deeds.

23

But today Gassire was greater than Gassire!"
The heroes rode behind Gassire into the city.
They sang:
    "Never before has Wagadu taken
    so many spears as today."
In the city Gassire was honored.
But when the men gathered,
Gassire did not join them.
Gassire wandered into the fields.
He heard the guinea hens.
Gassire drew close to them.
A guinea hen sat upon a bush and sang:
    "Hear the Dausi!
    Hear my deeds!"
The guinea hen sang of its battle with the snake.
The guinea hen sang:
    "All creatures must die, be buried, and vanish.
    Kings and heroes die, are buried, and vanish.
    I, too, shall die, shall be buried, and vanish.
    But the Dausi,
        the song of my battles,
        shall not die.
    It shall be sung again and again.
    It shall outlive all kings and heroes.
    Hoooh! that I might do such deeds!
    Hoooh! that I might sing the Dausi!
    Wagadu will be lost,
    But the Dausi shall endure and live!"

Hoooh!

    Dierra, Agada, Gana, Silla!

Hoooh!

    Fasa!

Gassire went again to the old wise man.

"Kiekorro!

    I was in the fields.

    I understood the guinea hens.

    The guinea hen boasted that the song of its deeds
would outlive Wagadu.

    The guinea hen sang the Dausi.

    Tell me,

        Are there men who know the Dausi?

        And can the Dausi last beyond life and death?"

The wise man said:

    "Gassire, you are rushing to meet your fate.

    No one can stop you.

    And since you will not be a king,

        you shall be a bard.

    Ah, Gassire!

    When the kings of the Fasa lived by the sea,

        they were also great heroes then.

    They fought against men who carried lutes,

        men who sang the Dausi.

    The Dausi of the enemy often struck terror

        into the hearts of the Fasa,

        who were themselves heroes.

26

But the Fasa never sang the Dausi,
    because they were of the first rank,
        the Horro.
The Dausi could be sung
    only by those of the second rank,
        the Diaru.
The Diaru fought
    not so much as warriors,
    to win the battle of the day,
but as drinkers,
    to relish the fame of the evening.
But you, Gassire,
    now that you will no longer be
        the second of the first,
    now shall you be
        the first of the second.
And Wagadu will be lost because of it."
And Gassire answered:
    "Then let Wagadu be lost!"
Hoooh!
    Dierra, Agada, Gana, Silla!
Hoooh!
    Fasa!

Gassire sought out a smith.
He said:
    "Make me a lute."
And the smith said:

"I will make you a lute.
But it will not sing."
Gassire said:
"Smith, you do your work.
The rest is my affair."
The smith made the lute.
He brought the lute to Gassire.
Gassire seized the lute.
He struck upon it.
The lute did not sound.
Gassire said:
"What is this?
The lute does not sing."
And the smith replied:
"I told you it would not.
I have done my work.
The rest is your affair."
Gassire asked:
"What must I do then?"
The smith spoke:
"The lute is but a piece of wood.
Without a heart it cannot sing.
You must give it a heart.
Carry the wood on your back when you go to battle.
The wood must ring with the strokes of your sword.
The wood must absorb the blood of your blood,
the breath of your breath.
Your pain must be its pain.
Your fame its fame.

The lute cannot then be just the wood of a tree.
It must blend with you and your people.
Therefore it must live not only with you,
        but with your sons.
Then the singing that comes from your heart
    will echo in the ear of your son
    and live on in your people.
And your son's life blood, oozing from his heart,
    will live on in this piece of wood.
Only then will it sound.
But Wagadu will be lost because of it."
Gassire said:
    "Then let Wagadu be lost!"
Hoooh!
    Dierra, Agada, Gana, Silla!
Hoooh!
    Fasa!

Gassire called his eight sons.
    "My sons, today we go to battle.
    But the strokes of our swords shall echo
        not only through the Sahel,
        but shall ring for the ages.
    You and I, my sons, will live on.
    We shall outlive all other heroes.
    We shall live on in the Dausi.
    My eldest son, today we two,
    You and I, will be first in the combat."

Gassire placed the lute over his shoulder.
And together with his eldest son went first into the field.
They charged the Burdama.
Gassire and his eldest son fought as the first.
They left the other heroes far behind them.
Gassire fought not like a human being,
      but like a Damo.
His eldest son fought not like a human being,
      but like a Damo.
In the thick of the fighting
   Gassire was hard-pressed by eight Burdama.
His son came swiftly to his side
   and struck four of them down.
Then one of the Burdama thrust a spear through his heart.
Gassire's eldest son fell dead from his horse.
In his rage, Gassire gave a great shout.
And the Burdama fled.
Gassire dismounted and lifted the body of his son
   upon his back.
Then he mounted and turned,
      and rode slowly back to the other heroes.
The heart's blood of his eldest son dropped,
      dropped onto the lute.
Thus Gassire, at the head of his heroes,
      rode into Dierra.
Hoooh!
      Dierra, Agada, Gana, Silla!
Hoooh!
      Fasa!

Gassire's eldest son was buried as a hero.
And all Dierra mourned.
That night Gassire took his lute
   and struck against the wood.
Still the lute did not sing.
Gassire's anger mounted.
He called his sons and said:
      "Tomorrow we ride again to combat."
For seven days Gassire rode with the heroes to battle.
And every day he took one of his sons with him
   to be the first in the fighting.
And on every one of these days
      Gassire carried the body of one of his sons
      over his shoulder and over the lute
      as they rode back into the city.
Thus, at the end of every day
      the blood of one of his sons
      dropped onto the lute.
After the seven days of fighting
   there was great mourning in Dierra.
All the heroes and all the women
   wore their mourning clothes of red and white.
All the women wailed.
All the men were angry.
Before the eighth day of the fighting
      all the heroes of Dierra gathered
      and they spoke to Gassire:
"Gassire, this must come to an end.

We fight willingly, but only as we must.
In your rage, you go on fighting
   without need, and without end.
Now go forth from Dierra!
Take those who would join you.
Take your slaves and your cattle.
As for us, we desire more of life than fame.
And while we should not like to live fameless,
  we have no wish to die for fame alone."
And the old wise man said:
  "Ah, Gassire!
  Thus will Wagadu be lost today for the first time
  because of your vanity."
Hoooh!
  Dierra, Agada, Gana, Silla!
Hoooh!
  Fasa!

Then rode Gassire out into the desert.
And with him rode his last, his youngest, son.
And his wives, his friends, his slaves, and his cattle.
They rode through the Sahel.
The heroes who had fought beside Gassire
  rode with him
   through the gates of the city.
Then many turned back.
But some followed Gassire and his son
  into the Sahara.

They traveled far.
Day and night they rode.
They came into the wilderness.
And there in the loneliness, they rested.
All slept: all the heroes, the women, the slaves.
Gassire's youngest son slept.
But Gassire himself did not sleep.
Gassire sat alone by the fire, listening.
Then close beside him, Gassire heard a voice.
The lute was sounding!
It rang as though it came from within himself.
Gassire listened and trembled,
        as the lute sang the Dausi.

When the lute had sung the Dausi
        for the first time,
King Nganamba died in the city, Dierra.
When the lute had sung the Dausi
        for the first time,
Gassire's rage melted; Gassire wept.
When the lute had sung the Dausi
        for the first time,
Wagadu was lost
        for the first time.
Hoooh!
        Dierra, Agada, Gana, Silla!
Hoooh!
        Fasa!

Four times
  Wagadu rose.
  A great city, gleaming in the light of day.
Four times
  Wagadu fell.
  And disappeared from human sight.
    Once through vanity.
    Once through dishonesty.
    Once through greed.
    Once through discord.
Four times
  Wagadu changed her name.
    First she was called Dierra,
      then Agada,
      then Gana,
      then Silla.
Four times
  Wagadu turned about,
    facing first to the north,
    then to the west,
    then to the east,
    then to the south.
Four gates
  have always led into Wagadu.
  Thus men have always seen them.
    One to the north.
    One to the west.
    One to the east, and

one to the south.
From these directions
Comes the strength of Wagadu.
Her power, which endures
Whether she be built of stone,
of wood, or
of earth.
Or whether she lives only as a shadow
In the memory and hopes of her children.
For in truth, Wagadu is not of stone,
not of wood,
nor of earth.
Wagadu is the strength
Which lives in the hearts of men.
Sometimes she becomes known
when men's eyes see her,
and their ears hear
the clash of swords and the clang of shields.
Sometimes lost to view,
when wearied and oppressed
by the strife of men,
she sleeps.
For the first time
Sleep came to Wagadu through vanity.
The second time through dishonesty.
The third time through greed.
The fourth time through discord.
Should Wagadu ever rise again,
She will live with such power

in the minds of men
            that she can never again be lost.
She will endure with such strength
        that vanity,
            dishonesty,
                greed,
                    discord,
        can never again harm her.
Hoooh!
        Dierra, Agada, Gana, Silla!
Hoooh!
        Fasa!

Each time Wagadu was destroyed
        through the faults of men,
She reappeared with a greater splendor.
Vanity brought the song of the bards.
Dishonesty brought a shower of gold and precious stones.
Greed brought the art of writing to the women of Wagadu.
The fifth Wagadu will arise from discord
        to endure as the rain of the South,
            as the rocks of the Sahara.
Every man then will bear Wagadu in his heart.
Every woman will have Wagadu in her sons.
Hoooh!
        Dierra, Agada, Gana, Silla!
Hoooh!
        Fasa!

GLOSSARY

Agada: The second Wagadu. Its location is unknown, though Frobenius suggests, on the slenderest evidence, that it was the oasis of Agades in the central Sahara.

Bard: In the Western Sudan, spoken literature has been kept alive and flourishing by special castes of minstrels and bards, for whom the general term is *griot.* They are trained from childhood in the traditional poetic and narrative forms, and are marvelously skillful in adapting them to contemporary use. The *griot* is a poet, singer, entertainer; the remembrancer of the old ways and commentator and satirist of the new.

Boroma: The Soninke name for the Fulani. They are also called Fula, Peuhl, Fulbe, or Bororo. At the time of which our legend speaks (presumably before the beginning of the Christian Era), the Fulani were a subject people of both the Soninke and the Tuareg. According to Frobenius, they fled south after the fall of the Fasa dynasty, and there lived independently. At present they number about seven million and are distributed throughout the Western Sudan as pagan migratory cattle herders or Muslim farmers and town dwellers.

Burdama: The Soninke name for the Tuareg, a Berber tribe of the Sahara Desert. They are exclusively camel pastoralists and traders, disdaining any form of agriculture. The Tuareg men are renowned both as warriors and as trans-Saharan caravan guides.

Calabash guitar: The native term for this instrument is the *kora*. It is a cross between a harp and a guitar. The base and sound box is half a large gourd covered with stretched goatskin. The twenty-one strings of twisted antelope hide are plucked or strummed by Sudanese musicians to produce a soft, melodic sound.

Caste: Soninke society has been described as a caste system, with the hereditary nobility at the top and, until recently, slaves at the bottom. Between these were the various occupational groups such as smiths, leather workers, and *griots*. They practice no other craft than the one assigned to them by tradition and caste membership, and marry only within their own castes. Talented and ambitious craftsmen may achieve wealth, but can never move up into the ranks of the *Horro*. When Gassire opted for the lute instead of his father's sword and shield, he was clearly cutting himself and his descendants off from the prerogatives of nobility forever.

Damo: This is probably an archaic word. Frobenius's informant used it freely, but could not explain its meaning. I would hazard a guess that it refers to some overpowering spiritual being or force.

Dausi: The whole of a long and continuous epic recounting the rise and fall of Soninke fortunes. It was probably created no later than the seventeenth century out of many existing separate historical legends, folktales, and songs. Only scattered fragments are remembered and recited now by the bards. *Gassire's Lute* is the keystone legend of the *Dausi*, since it accounts for its origin among the Soninke.

Diari: The Soninke word for their bards. If our legend is to be believed, the *Diaru* (plural form) were of noble origin, but are now a separate caste dependent upon noble patronage. Another Soninke term for their bards is *Geseri* (*Geseru*—plural), probably derived from Gassire, the legendary founder of the Soninke bardic tradition and caste.

Dierra: The first Wagadu, ruled by the Fasa dynasty. There is no real evidence as to its location. Frobenius assumes it was Djerma, on the site of the present oasis of Murzuq in the Fezzan, but more likely it was much farther south in the Sahel.

Fasa: The ruling dynasty of Dierra. It obviously refers to a hereditary lineage or clan of nobles. Frobenius says the name was taken from the Fezzan, where they originated.

Gana (Ghana): The third Wagadu, probably the great Soninke kingdom of the fourth to the thirteenth centuries, located between the Senegal and Niger rivers. The term "Gana" referred originally to the title of the Soninke kings, but was extended to mean the entire kingdom. Gana achieved the peak of its prosperity and expansion in the tenth century, mostly through its commercial control of the salt and gold traffic across the Sahara. It succumbed finally under the repeated attacks of Muslims from North Africa, and the depredations of its neighbors, the Tuareg and the Fulani. Gana was vividly described by the Arab chronicler El-Bekri in 1067 as a wealthy and powerful state. Three hundred years later, another Arab, Ibn Khaldun, described its ruin.

Gassire: The legendary founder of the bardic tradition and of the *griot* caste among the Soninke. He was of the noble line of the Fasa kings. (The name is pronounced Gahséereh, with the accent on the stressed syllable.)

Horro: The Soninke word designating the caste of nobles and rulers. Noble rank exists only within certain family lines. *Horro* families still take great pride in their rank and lineage, even though the prerogatives of nobility have mostly disappeared.

Nganámba: The last Soninke king of the Fasa dynasty. (The initial "ng," common to many African languages, is pronounced much as we pronounce the "ng" in ri*ng*. The vowel sounds are pronounced as the "a" in f*a*ther. The accent marks the stressed syllable.)

Pui: Soninke poems and songs about the brave deeds of particular heroes. There is a legend that seems closely related to *Gassire's Lute,* telling of the origin of the Pui: The guinea hen has laid many large and beautiful eggs of which she is justly proud. As she goes out to forage for food, a giant snake comes by and swallows all her eggs. The guinea hen is thoroughly roused, and decides, in her anger, to declare war against the snake. She sets out in pursuit of the snake, and to build up her courage for the martial undertaking, sings a song of war and vengeance. Gassire, who understands the song of birds, hears her song and follows the guinea hen. He observes her encounter with the snake, her battle and subsequent victory. Then the bird flies to a tree and sings of her brave deed. Her song was the first *Pui*, and Gassire learned it and sang it to the people. (From L. Frobenius, *Spielmannsgeschichten der Sahel*.)

Sahel: A narrow belt of grassland that extends along the southern edge of the Sahara. Soninkeland is in the West Sahel. In much earlier times the Sahel probably provided fairly good grazing, but the Sahara has been steadily encroaching upon the grassland for centuries, and it is now a semi-arid area, barely able to support the herds of cattle that the Soninke value so highly.

Silla: The fourth Wagadu. A small city-state on the west bend of the Niger. Formerly more important, it is now a town in Soninkeland.

Slave: Until recently slaves existed in Soninke society. Originally acquired as captives of war or by purchase, slaves occupied the bottom rungs of Soninke life. Those born in Soninke households enjoyed a more privileged position, and after several generations they might become free men.

Smith: A separate occupational caste in Soninke society. Smiths are all considered to be magicians as well. Thus the smith in *Gassire's Lute* naturally incorporated magical properties into the lute that he made.

Soninke: A tribe of the Western Sudan numbering a half-million people. They are also called Sarakolle (with various spellings), Serahuli, and Marka. In the Senegambian area, *Soninke*, meaning "drinkers of fermented liquor," was applied to the warrior groups who remained loyal to the pagan states after the rise of Islam. Now the Soninke are mostly Muslim. Most of the information available on Soninke culture is in the work of French anthropologists: M. Delafosse, *Haut-Sénégal-Niger*, 3 vols. (Paris: 1912); Henri Labouret, *Paysans d'Afrique occidentale* (Paris: 1941); C. Monteil, *La Légende du Ouagadou...* (Dakar: 1953); L. J. B. Saint-Père, *Les Sarakollé du Guinimakha* (Paris: 1925).

Wagadu: A Soninke word meaning "place of herds." At present it refers to a small area in the Western Sahel that is inhabited mainly by Soninke. It was the name the Soninke gave from earliest times to whatever area they considered their homeland.

Writing: The art of writing that came with the rise of the fourth Wagadu probably refers to the introduction of *Tifinagh* to the Soninke. *Tifinagh* is a presumably very ancient Berber script now used only by the Tuareg. The letters consist mostly of enclosed lines and dots, and can be written starting from either the left or right, or running upward or downward. It was probably more a form of bookkeeping than literature. The Tuareg women were particularly skilled in its use. Contact between the Tuareg and Soninke, though usually hostile in nature, was nonetheless continuous over many centuries. It is not inconceivable that traits of culture should pass between them, and that one as remarkable as *Tifinagh* should be immortalized in Soninke legend.

THE ORIGIN OF SONINKE BARDIC ART

Anthropologists and folklorists as well as students of literature have affirmed the basic and long-held idea that the narrative and poetic forms of a culture confirm its values and validate its social systems. In his classic work on mythology, the highly esteemed anthropologist Bronislaw Malinowski stressed the point that myth is a charter for the institutions of society.[1] The well-known folklorist Alan Dundes stated that folklore represents the world view of the society from which it came.[2] All writers on the subject hold that myth and folklore constitute a vital form of communication conveying all kinds of information, from the esoteric aspects of religion to the everyday rules of etiquette, and much in between. Another fruitful dimension has been added to the study of folklore in newer approaches which stress performance within a social context, emphasizing the processes, the ''how'' of communication, rather than content alone.[3]

Much folklore, however, exists as a tremendous backlog of content from which the current performance aspects cannot be deduced. Volumes of myth and folklore texts from non-European cultures sit on library shelves, neatly bound, many untranslated and many unread. Yet they are a valuable resource that anthropologists and folklorists cannot dismiss. These older materials should be restudied with a view to whatever light they may shed on the total communication process.

In much of the folklore collected in the past we are confronted by text and content, with little, if any, knowledge of context. Both text and content have been filtered and diluted through time and translation. It is possible, nonetheless, in some instances to reconstruct certain aspects of context, imagery, and even world view from contemporaneous historical and ethnographic accounts, or to adduce these aspects from current data. Aside from its content (the story of the fall of Dierra, the prince who became a bard, the epic battles with traditional enemies, the origin of the ''Dausi,'' and so on), a careful reexamination of *Gassire's Lute* provided me with some context such as information concerning Soninke social patterns, the caste system, dynastic successions, magic and warfare. Most significantly, it yielded an image of the performer, the bard as an integral component of context. And it is an unexpected image, one that is atypical for a traditional society.

The Soninke

We have astonishingly little current information concerning the Soninke despite the fact that they are the oldest population with historical tradition in the Sahel. The sum of that knowledge can be gathered from a few old monographs of localized populations, a few legends, and accounts from early Arab traders. Their original greatness stems from the empire of Ghana, which even today is regarded as a crowning achievement of ancient Africa. The modern nation of Ghana, though distant in time and place from ancient Ghana, was named in tribute to the ancient glory of the empire. There had been, before the culmination of Soninke power in Ghana, other political entities over which the Soninke ruled, though none of these were as vast or as wealthy as Ghana. The early Soninke were basically farmers, growing the food plants of the Sudanic area such as millet, sorghum and ground peas. Some were skilled craftsmen in leather, cloth and metal. They had acquired knowledge of mining, smelting and forging several centuries B.C. Above all, they were traders. Situated at the convergence of the great trans-Saharan trade routes, they saw the advantage of taxing the passage of goods as well as trading them for their own produce. It was this that made them wealthy and powerful enough to control and regulate the trade in gold from the southwest forest areas of West Africa, and the trade in salt from the northern Saharan mines. One might say that they were in the right place at the right time, for along with gold and salt came many other desirable items: slaves and ivory from the south and manufactured articles from the Mediterranean world.

The power of the Soninke lasted nearly a thousand years. But from the eighth to the thirteenth centuries, the empire suffered a succession of disasters: prolonged drought, invasions, and finally the conquest of Ghana by the Maninke (Mandingo) kingdom of Mali. Each of these depredations precipitated a Soninke dispersal into other parts of West Africa. They are no longer a separate, bounded kingdom or a country, but today can be found spread throughout West and Equatorial Africa where they are traders or migrant workers. There is evidence that many of the wandering Soninke mingled with and were finally absorbed by other populations such as the Wolof and the Maninke. Some settled in the Ivory Coast, where they constitute a wealthy and influential minority. Bamako, a large city on the Niger River in Mali contains a population of Soninke who are regarded as the most important and innovative traders of printed cloth and livestock.

The Diari or Gesere

Gassire's Lute is a fragment of an ancient Soninke epic that purports to recount Soninke dynastic history, and, indeed, Leo Frobenius, who collected it in 1909 from a Soninke bard living in northern Dahomey, attempts to reconstruct from the content the circumstances of Soninke dynastic successions, dispersions, and migrations in the time-honored anthropological response to such legends.[4] His reconstruction is highly dubious: he does not allow for distortion in transmission over time, for the vagaries of faulty memory or personal performance style, or for the need for national self-glorification to which legend is heir. His version of *Gassire's Lute* does not permit an accurate historical view of the Soninke past in those terms that Frobenius sought.

Lacking Frobenius's original notes, it is not possible to ascertain the accuracy of his translation. Nor can I establish with any degree of certainty meter, phonological patterns, rhythms, or whether the legend was chanted or sung. In fact, direct evidence for most aspects of the social context in which the epic might be transmitted is lacking. The manner of delivery, intonations, and pauses can be deduced only from modern analogues of the old Soninke bards — the current *griots* of modern Africa. Frobenius provides some information on the old Soninke bards, the *diari*, also called *gesere*. These performing artists were repositories of tribal lore. Their song and stories described the ancient days of chivalry when each noble (*horro*) youth, his knightly training completed, was given a horse, weapons, his own *diaru*, and sent off to make his mark on the world. Always at the side of the *horro* warrior rode his *diaru*, who was never counted as a servant, but a friend, wise counselor, and praise singer. The Soninke code of honor did not permit the knight to boast of his own deeds, but he could count on his *diaru* to do his boasting for him. The *diaru*'s songs extolling his lord's courage, daring, and devotion to honor spread over the western Sudan.

The Soninke *diari*, then, did not differ in their function from the other *griots* and praise singers of the western Sudan. They everywhere form a special caste, trained from child-hood in traditional poetic and narrative forms, adept at reworking them to contemporary usage. Throughout the area the *griot* is the poet, singer, and entertainer; he is the remembrancer of the old ways and the commentator and satirist of the new. What distinguished the Soninke *diaru* is that he was viewed as an artist, a full professional, and that he enjoyed high status, just beneath that of the *horro*. In the legend, Gassire was told by the diviner that in forfeiting the kingship he would no longer be first among the *horro*, the noble caste, but first of the *diaru*, the second caste. This change in rank represents, at least in modern West Africa, a major reduction in status. There is no precedent for Gassire's possible reactions, but among the Soninke the *horro* had, and still have, an elevated image. Not only are they aristocrats, but they are above all caste rankings. Gassire would have been giving up a great deal.

Anthropologists have described performers similar to the Soninke *griots* all over Africa, though their roles and position in society and their attitudes toward their art vary greatly. In northern Nigeria, among the Hausa, the occupation of musician has always ranked low and is regarded as a craft. While originality and improvisational skill are admired, the musicians are viewed as good technicians rather than as artists. David Ames comments that "the notion of producing art for the love of it is notable for its absence in the outlook of the majority of Hausa musicians; rather they have a commercial attitude, or perhaps more correctly, a craftsman's mentality. Their music is viewed purely and simply as the means for earning their bread. Most informants indicated that they would not play for their own pleasure if they shifted to another occupation and some asked what would be the use of it."[5]

Alan Merriam tells us that among the Bala of Zaire, the status of musician was also extremely low, but approximates the Soninke somewhat in that musicians are nonetheless important to the society despite their low position. "They keep the village happy and though as individuals they are scorned, life without musicians is not to be considered."[6]

Professional storytellers and musicians, players of the *akpata* (bow-lute) and *asologun* (thumb piano) in Benin are regarded as social isolates. In Dan Ben-Amos's account they emerge as introverted and depressed figures whose skilled performances give pleasure but provide only minimal financial rewards. Ben-Amos describes the instruments themselves and their players as "associated with outcast figures in both the religious and political structures — the witches, the spirits of the night and the unsuccessful rulers." The *asologun* in particular is regarded as the instrument of the witches, and its use is banned entirely in Benin City and by many local chiefs as well.[7]

Geoffrey Gorer barely mentions the Wolof *griot* in his *Africa Dances*, but he does indicate that they were slaves, attached to noble households.[8] David Gamble reaffirms this statement about the Wolof, but makes additional mention of *griots* who were not slaves, but a freeborn musician's caste of low rank even below the smith, and that such *griots* might amass great wealth, even having their own *griot* slaves.[9]

54

Status is a matter of some importance in the context of performance, as is self-image. The deference of an audience to a high-caste performer adds further dimension to the performance itself. A slave *griot* can only sing praises or veiled insults of his master; a freeborn and aristocratic performer has far greater latitude in performing traditional material and in creating new material.

According to Claude Meillassoux, the Soninke bardic tradition still persists in attenuated form in the city of Bamako. The *gesere* or *diari* still function as bards, musicians, and genealogists. They are used in Bamako and its rural environs as intermediaries in courtship and often in diplomacy. They live on gifts from the *horro* and, indeed, "are not ashamed to ask for them." Their abilities as praise singers and their assured access to the public has given them an independence of spirit and a reputation of being feared by those who pay them. They may as easily malign as praise. This, in itself, is sufficient reason for paying them well. A few, however, have established themselves as successful and independent performers, singing on the radio or for record companies. Also based in Bamako is the Association des Artistes du Mali, a national organization of performers. A Soninke *gesere* is one of its leading officials, and others are members. Its performances are lavish affairs, including speech making, dancing, and drumming. They often end with the performance of a "kind of verse chronicle, called *fasa*, sung by a famous griot accompanied by a *kora* (calabash guitar) player."[10] It is possible that *Gassire's Lute* in some form is part of this chronicle. The name *Fasa* is that of Gassire's dynasty. Apart from this brief statement, Meillassoux says nothing about the *fasa*, the performance, or its content. And this remains the only hint in the literature that the legend is remembered or performed at all. Clearly only fieldwork can resolve these problems concerning the present-day performance of traditional Soninke legends, and the problems of original performance style or in Frobenius's time will simply have to remain unanswered or as educated guesses.

Gassire's Lute: The Epic

Gassire's Lute recommends itself to special scrutiny because it has, even in German translation, the quality of epic poetry, lending itself to stanzas, structured by formal repetition of words and ideas, and rhythmic sentence structure. The highly sophisticated structure of *Gassire's Lute* does not seem to have direct analogues in other West African folklore. It can, perhaps, be explained by Arabic contacts, or what is more likely, both contact and the endless refining and reworking of this key legend by a long succession of generations of Soninke bards. And along with the Mandekan epic of Sun Jiata, the great leader and founder of the Mali empire, *Gassire's Lute* clearly demonstrates the presence of the heroic epic in West Africa.[11]

It is tantalizing to have so little annotative information concerning the performers and performance of such legends. Isidore Okpewho's scholarly work on the African epic establishes the importance of the epic tradition in Africa, and although the author mentions the crucial place of context and performance in epic studies, he is far more concerned with textual material than the details of either performers or performance.[12] I would give a great deal to have the kind of data on these matters with which the scholars Daniel Biebuyck and Kahombo C. Mateene preface the lengthy and detailed Mwindo epic from the Congolese Banyanga.[13] However, internal evidence from *Gassire's Lute* itself leads to the assumption that it retains

56

integrity as a model of the *dausi*, the epic poetry chanted by the Soninke bards to the accompaniment of the lute (*kora*).

The narrative structure of the epic itself forms a triple frame. The first frame deals with the rise and fall of the Soninke city-states. This part of the narrative is entirely repeated both as prologue and again as epilogue. The historical segments bracket the tale of Gassire's transformation from the last warrior-prince of the Fasa dynasty to the first Soninke bard. Thus, from being a member of the *horro* caste, he becomes a member of the *diari* or *gesere* caste. This section, in turn, frames still another, smaller legend of the victory of the guinea fowl over the snake. While the guinea fowl proclaims this victory as the subject for a great epic poem, or *dausi*, Frobenius mentions that it is an example of another, lesser poetic form called the *pui*. These are individual songs or chants which exalt the feats of particular heroes. They are chanted in regular meter with specifically set melodic accompaniment. There is another Soninke legend which tells of the origin of the *pui*. It may, in fact, be still another fragment of the *dausi*, disconnected from the original narrative matrix, distorted over time, and reworked to account for the existence of the *pui*. It tells the story of the victory of the hen over the snake. Gassire, understanding the language of animals, incorporated it into his *dausi*.

The prologue of the tale of Gassire tells that Wagadu, the Soninke state, existed four times, each time being lost through human error, and that when it rises for the last time, it will never again fall. The narrative then recounts the fall of the first Wagadu and the destruction of the Fasa dynasty. Gassire, the warrior-son of the ailing old king, cannot contain his impatience to rule. His battles in a

57

continuous and bloody war with the Tuareg and Fulani, both nomadic, warlike tribes of the area are described, as is his yearning to be king. Upon consulting a diviner, he is told that his fate is never to rule over Wagadu but to be the first Soninke to sing the *dausi*. Granted the power to understand the speech of birds, he hears the guinea fowl chant the *dausi* of her triumph over the snake and is overwhelmed by their statement that the *dausi* will outlive them and all ephemera.

Again consulting the diviner, Gassire becomes obsessed with the everlasting glory of the *dausi* and is told that he, too, will create such art, but that in doing so he will lose his kingdom, and the Soninke city will be destroyed. A lute is fashioned for him, but it will not sound. The diviner then tells him that the lute will play only when the player has given up both his ambition to rule and the glories of battle, when his life's blood mingles with the wood of the lute, when he has sacrificed his sons and his worldly ambition. When he and the lute are one, only then will it respond to his song and only then can he sing the *dausi*, which will last forever.

It is a tragic epic, for now swayed solely by his compulsion to create the timeless art of the *dausi*, Gassire sacrifices his patrimony, his rule, his city, and his sons. He is driven out of the city to wander in the desert. There in the loneliness and solitude, all else relinquished, the lute sounds, and Gassire's *dausi* is created. He is ruthless in his sacrifice; yet our sympathies are engaged. He is the poet we know from our own cultural perceptions, almost maddened by the obsession to create an art that will outlast him.

The creators of the epic were wonderfully perceptive of certain kinds of human behavior. They saw clearly the havoc that could be wrought by unbridled egotism, that the monumental obsession of the artist would obviate the social responsibility required of a political leader. This is a familiar theme in Western culture. Our own literature and history have provided us with many examples of people as single-minded in their dedication to art.

While Gassire may have abjured his noble birth and caused the fall of the first Wagadu, he is nonetheless perceived as a true culture hero. Out of the destruction and tragedy he brought the art of minstrelsy to his people, and the descendants of his line, though no longer kings of Soninke, became its bards.

The Romantic Aesthetic

Gassire's Lute is an important legend in that it explains for the Soninke the background for their diaspora, but its greater significance for our purposes lies in their conception of the Soninke *diaru*. Their view forces us to expand a Western Romantic aesthetic to include a nonliterate population. The art historian Harold Osborne describes the European artist of the Romantic period as a "person with an abnormally strong sense of vocation, one who labors under an obsessive feeling of compulsion which is expressed in an anguished need to realize latent capacities — to be oneself — or to discover some transcendental and inexpressible truth."[14] The phenomena of compulsion, a sense of rightness, and the relief which can only be derived through achievement is thus not limited to the artists of the Western world. These are all aspects of Gassire's personality as described in the legend, and Gassire is the prototype of the Soninke artist. Before him there were no Soninke bards, and his compulsion toward greatness, toward self-expression, leads him from the honors of war and rule to the immortality conferred by singing the *dausi* and, incidentally, becoming the eponymous hero of an entire caste named *gesere*. The driving need for self-realization, obsessive, and almost outside himself, leads him to sacrifice his kingdom and his sons. Inexorably he fulfilled the diviner's prophecy:

> The lute is but a piece of wood.
> Without a heart it cannot sing.
> You must give it a heart.
> Carry the wood on your back when you go to battle.
> The wood must ring with the strokes of your sword.
> The wood must absorb the blood of your blood,
>   the breath of your breath.
> Your pain must be it pain.
>   Your fame its fame.
> The lute cannot then be just the wood of a tree.
> It must blend with you and your people.
> Therefore it must live not only with you, but with your sons.
> Then the singing that comes from your heart will echo in the
>   ear of your son and live on in your people.
> And your son's life blood, oozing from his heart will live on
>   in this piece of wood.
>   Only then will it sound.

The legend is also, then, the charter for the alienation of the artist from the binding obligations of other members of society. The Western Romantic concept of the artist stresses his need, not for the ties of kind and the bonds of human relationships, but the freedom to create his art unburdened by the mundane cares of the world. Society will tolerate much from the creative artist. His creativity brings beauty and understanding, and for that his people will accept antisocial behavior. The Soninke sorrowed at the death of Gassire's seven sons, at his unceasing war with the enemy and with himself; but finally, for his unreasoning behavior and his filicide, he was literally cast out of society. He had gone too far, and they could no longer condone his madness. He was ordered to leave. While this is the archetypal form of self-sacrifice for one's art, it also symbolizes the freedom of the artist from the constrictions of "normal" society, and it holds out the possibility of creativity outside its bounds.

> Gassire, this must come to an end.
> We fight willingly, but only as we must.
> In your rage, you go on fighting
>   Without need and without end.
> Now go forth from Dierra.
> As for us, we desire more of life than fame.
> And while we should not like to live fameless
>   we have no wish to die for fame alone.

Gassire's obsession shifts from his overweening desire to be king to the need to create the *dausi* that will confer immortality on him and his line. This was equally the motivation of the Romantic artists of the Western world. They, too, sought immortality in their works. In Blake's *Vision of the Last Judgment*, the exegesis of the Romantic ideal is that art transcends the artist, empiricism, and the confines of time and experience. The same vision of the immortality of art was manifested even earlier in the work of Renaissance artists, and Shakespeare's sonnets, especially Sonnet 18, describe the ephemeral nature of love and life itself, "but so long as man can breathe and eyes can see, so long lives *this*, and *this* gives life to thee."

Probably the most interesting and significant parallel between the Soninke ideal and that of the Western Romantic movement is the concept of art as self-expression. The whole of biographical and sociological criticism is based on the assumption that the work of art expresses directly the character of the artist, or that it provides a means for ventilation of submerged personality traits. Gassire's need for self-expression is the reason the city fell, the first Soninke hegira undertaken, and a new art form created. His

61

personality is the focus of the legend, and his obsession with fame and immortality are front stage center as his motivation.

This essay would seem to invoke many more questions than answers. I would not advocate building a cultural ideology or artistic aesthetic on any one artifact. Nor can I explain how a presumably medieval art form (bardism) embodies a Romantic formulation of the artist, or how a European aesthetic is bound to a non-European art form, unless Frobenius distorted the legend out of all reasonable bounds. This seems unlikely, however, in view of the richness of content in the legend. Yet, if folk art represents a world view, we may assume that *Gassire's Lute* as an artistic item conveys the Soninke perception of the artist, and it is a strangely unexpected view. The Soninke *diaru* emerges from this epic as a counterpart to the Romantic Western notion of the artist, with the world well lost for art.

Notes

This paper is a revised and expanded version of a paper presented at the meetings of the New York African Studies Association in April 1978, and published in *Research in African Literatures*. Vol. 15, No. 4, pp. 519-529, 1984.

1. Bronislaw Malinowski, "Myth in Primitive Psychology" in *Magic, Science and Religion and Other Essays*, Garden City, NY: Doubleday and Co., 1954.

2. Alan Dundes, "Folk Ideas as Units of World View," in *Towards New Perspectives in Folklore*, ed. A. Paredes and R. Bauman (Austin: University of Texas Press, 1972), pp. 93-103.

3. Roger D. Abrahams, "Personal Power and Social Restraint," pp. 16-30, and Dan Ben-Amos, "Toward a Definition of Folklore in Context," pp. 3-15, in *Towards New Perspectives in Folklore*, ed. A. Paredes and R. Bauman (Austin: University of Texas Press, 1972). Also see

Richard Bauman, "Towards a Behavioral Theory of Folklore: A Reply to Roger Welsch," *Journal of American Folklore*, 82 (1969), 167-70, and idem, "Verbal Art as Performance," *American Anthropologist*, 77 (1975), 290-311.

4. Leo Frobenius in *Speilmanns-Geschichten der Sahel*, Atlantis, Bd. VI (Jena: E. Diederichs Verlag, 1921).

5. David W. Ames, "A Sociocultural View of Hausa Musical Activity," in *The Traditional Artist in African Societies*, ed.Warren L. D'Azevedo (Bloomington: Indiana University Press, 1973), p. 152.

6. Alan P. Merriam, "The Bala Musician," in *The Traditional Artist in African Societies*, ed. Warren L. D'Azevedo (Bloomington: Indiana University Press, 1973), p. 267.

7. Dan Ben-Amos, *Sweet Words: Storytelling Events in Benin* (Philadelphia: Institute for the Study of Human Issues, 1975), pp. 35-54.

8. Geoffrey Gorer, *Africa Dances* (New York: Norton Library, 1962).

9. David Gamble, *The Wolof of Senegambia* (London, International African Institute, 1957).

10. Claude Meillassoux, *Urbanization of an African Community* (Seattle, University of Washington Press, 1968).

11. See John W. Johnson, "*Yes, Virginia, There Is an Epic in Africa*," *Research in African Literatures*, 11 (Fall 1980), 309-26, for cogent arguments about the structure, content, and indeed, the existence of the heroic epic in Africa.

12. Isidore Okpewho, *The Epic in Africa* (New York: Columbia University Press, 1979).

13. Daniel Biebuyck and Kahombo C. Mateene, *The Mwindo Epic* (Berkeley and Los Angeles: University of California Press, 1969).

14. Harold Osborne, *Aesthetics and Art Theory* (New York: E.P. Dutton, 1970), p. 207.

ALTA JABLOW received her Ph.D. in anthropology from Columbia University and is now Professor Emerita, having retired from Brooklyn College, CUNY, where she taught anthropology and folklore for over thirty years. Dr. Jablow has done fieldwork among the Vai and Bassa peoples in Liberia, and taught at the University of Liberia in Monrovia. Her previous books are *Yes and No: The Folklore of West Africa*; *An Anthology of West African Folklore*; *Rainbow in the Morning* and *The Man in the Moon* (with Carl Withers); *The Africa That Never Was* and *Women in Cultures of the World* (with Dorothy Hammond). Dr. Jablow and her husband, who is also an anthropologist, live in New York City.

LEO and DIANE DILLON, internationally known, have been illustrating together for over thirty years. Their career has reflected cultural diversity. Twice they have been recipients of the Randolph Caldecott Award. Their most recent picture books are *Aida* by Leontyne Price and *Tale of the Mandarin Ducks* by Katherine Patterson.